WE LOVE CATS

By the same author

The Medicine Men (1975)
Paper Doctors (1976)
Everything You Want To Know About Ageing (1976)
Stress Control (1978)
The Home Pharmacy (1980)
Aspirin or Ambulance (1980)
Face Values (1981)
Guilt (1982)
The Good Medicine Guide (1982)
Stress And Your Stomach (1983)
Bodypower (1983)
An A to Z Of Women's Problems (1984)
Bodysense (1984)
Taking Care Of Your Skin (1984)
A Guide to Child Health (1984)
Life Without Tranquillisers (1985)
Diabetes (1985)
Arthritis (1985)
Eczema and Dermatitis (1985)
The Story Of Medicine (1985, 1998)
Natural Pain Control (1986)
Mindpower (1986)
Addicts and Addictions (1986)
Dr Vernon Coleman's Guide To Alternative Medicine (1988)
Stress Management Techniques (1988)
Overcoming Stress (1988)
Know Yourself (1988)
The Health Scandal (1988)
The 20 Minute Health Check (1989)
Sex For Everyone (1989)
Mind Over Body (1989)
Eat Green Lose Weight (1990)
Why Animal Experiments Must Stop (1991)
The Drugs Myth (1992)
How To Overcome Toxic Stress (1990)
Why Doctors Do More Harm Than Good (1993)
Stress and Relaxation (1993)
Complete Guide To Sex (1993)
How to Conquer Backache (1993)
How to Conquer Arthritis (1993)
Betrayal of Trust (1994)
Know Your Drugs (1994, 1997)

Food for Thought (1994)
The Traditional Home Doctor (1994)
I Hope Your Penis Shrivels Up (1994)
People Watching (1995)
Relief from IBS (1995)
The Parent's Handbook (1995)
Oral Sex: Bad Taste And Hard To Swallow? (1995)
Why Is Pubic Hair Curly? (1995)
Men in Dresses (1996)
Power over Cancer (1996)
Crossdressing (1996)
How To Get The Best Out Of Prescription Drugs (1996)
How To Get The Best Out of Alternative Medicine (1996)
How To Conquer Arthritis (1996)
High Blood Pressure (1996)
How To Stop Your Doctor Killing You (1996)
Fighting For Animals (1996)
Alice and Other Friends (1996)
Dr Coleman's Fast Action Health Secrets (1997)
Dr Vernon Coleman's Guide to Vitamins and Minerals (1997)
Spiritpower (1997)
Other People's Problems (1998)
How To Publish Your Own Book (1999)
How To Relax and Overcome Stress (1999)
Animal Rights – Human Wrongs (1999)
Superbody (1999)
The 101 Sexiest, Craziest, Most Outrageous Agony Column Questions
    (and Answers) of All Time (1999)
Strange But True (2000)
Food For Thought [revised edition] (2000)
Daily Inspirations (2000)
Stomach Problems: Relief At Last (2001)
How To Overcome Guilt (2001)
How To Live Longer (2001)

novels
The Village Cricket Tour (1990)
The Bilbury Chronicles (1992)
Bilbury Grange (1993)
Mrs Caldicot's Cabbage War (1993)
Bilbury Revels (1994)
Deadline (1994)
The Man Who Inherited a Golf Course (1995)
Bilbury Country (1996)

Second Innings (1999)
Around the Wicket (2000)
It's Never Too Late (2001)

short stories
Bilbury Pie (1995)

on cricket
Thomas Winsden's Cricketing Almanack (1983)
Diary Of A Cricket Lover (1984)

as Edward Vernon
Practice Makes Perfect (1977)
Practise What You Preach (1978)
Getting Into Practice (1979)
Aphrodisiacs – An Owner's Manual (1983)
Aphrodisiacs – An Owner's Manual (Turbo Edition) (1984)
The Complete Guide To Life (1984)

as Marc Charbonnier
Tunnel (novel 1980)

with Alice
Alice's Diary (1989)
Alice's Adventures (1992)

with Dr Alan C Turin
No More Headaches (1981)

WE LOVE CATS

Vernon Coleman

With illustrations by the author

Chilton Designs Publishers

First published in 2002 by Chilton Designs Publishers, Publishing House, Trinity Place, Barnstaple, Devon EX32 9HJ, England.

This book is copyright. Enquiries should be addressed to the author c/o the publishers.

Copyright © Vernon Coleman 2002. The right of Vernon Coleman to be identified as the author of this work has been asserted in accordance with the Copyright, Designs and Patents Act 1988.

Reprinted 2002

ISBN: 1 898146 50 0

A catalogue record for this book is available from the British Library.

Printed and bound by: J W Arrowsmith Limited, Bristol

Dedication and Acknowledgement

This book is primarily dedicated to my wife, Donna Antoinette (the Welsh Princess) with acknowledgement, thanks and cat-baskets full of love. Without her this book wouldn't exist. It was the Welsh Princess who dug out the facts, found the quotes, laughed just the right amount at my dodgy drawings, and helped with the silly rhymes when I got stuck. If this book was a film, a large stretch of the credits would carry the same name – hers. As a result, if there is any credit for this book my lovely Donna Antoinette should get a lion's share. (But if there is any blame go-ing I'll keep that to my-self, thank you very much.) The bit of the book that isn't dedicated to Donna Antoinette is dedicated to the memory of Alice, Dick, Harry, Thomasina, Timmy and Marmalade.

Note

As readers of my books *Alice's Diary* and *Alice's Adventures* will already know I often use the word 'Upright' instead of the phrase 'human being'.

Contents List

Paws for Thought

You and I have something important in common: we both love cats.

A love of cats transcends everything else. It doesn't matter how old you are, where you live or what you do with the rest of your life, we have a fundamental passion that draws us together: we're catfriends.

And so I hope you get as much pleasure out of this collection of catfacts, quotations, silly limericks and squiggly drawings and 'catoons' as I got out of putting it all together.

Vernon Coleman, Devon 2002

1
Quotes From Cats

'I always allow Uprights to sleep in their own bed. As long as they keep to the edge.'

Sooty (black and white cat aged 4)

'Some Uprights believe that cats choose inconvenient places to sit or lie either out of a sense of mischief or through simple thoughtlessness. This is a complete misconception. All properly educated cats know that choosing a position that is thoroughly inconvenient to their Upright is an essential part of the education process. Uprights have to be taught who is in charge. All cats should know the mathematical formula for working out the precise place to sit that will cause the greatest inconvenience. The basic formula $(p = x + y)$ for calculating the best position is simple. In this formula p is the position to be assessed, x stands for inconvenience to the Upright and y denotes comfort to the cat.'

Tiddles (mackerel tabby cat aged 11)

'Cats should be gentle with their Uprights – as long as their Uprights remember their places.'

Snowy (white cat aged 5)

'Always begin washing your face if threatened with a difficult or potentially embarrassing situation. This simple ploy never fails.'

Blackie (black cat aged 7)

'The quickest way to put an Upright in his or her place is to walk away and sit with your back to them. This almost never fails to produce an apology, a cuddle and a titbit or two.'

Missy (Blotched tabby cat aged 3)

'A door is a large piece of wood separating a cat from where it wants to be.'

Mogs (Tabby cat aged 8)

'Dogs are stupid, craven and subservient. A dog will sit beside his master while his master works; pathetically waiting for a scrap of attention. Any cat worth his or her salt will sit directly on the work so as to ensure that he or she receives the Upright's full and undivided attention.'

Fluffy (Chinchilla Persian cat aged 4)

2
Cats in the movies

The Odd Couple

The Magnificent Seven

The Prisoner

A Room with a View

The Great Escape

The Birds

Treasure Island

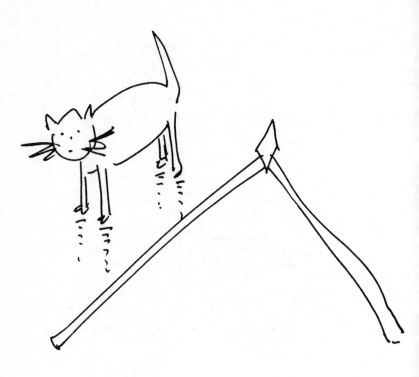

Cat on a Hot Tin Roof (1)

Cat on a Hot Tin Roof (2)

Singing in the Rain

The Sound of Music

Death in Venice

It's a Wonderful Life

Some Like It Hot

Catch Me If You Can

The Night of the Hunter

Three Men In A Boat

Vanity Fair

The Big Sleep

War and Peace

Great Expectations

The Sting

The Good, The Bad and The Ugly

3
Catmyths debunked by Marmalade

I've heard Uprights claim that we can heal ourselves by licking our wounds. I don't know where this non-sense came from but it's dangerous phooey. Licking a wound is more likely to do harm than good – making the wound worse and slowing down the body's own healing process. Like scratching an itch it's some-thing that is best discouraged.

One of the daftest things I've ever heard an Upright say is that cats who are neutered or spayed will inevitably put on weight. This is nonsense. It's like arguing that men who have vasec-tomies will always put on weight. It's true that most men who have vasectomies do put on weight – but the weight gain has nothing whatsoever to do with the surgery they've had on their delicate bits. Like Uprights, some cats of a certain age tend to put on weight because they eat too much and spend too much time slumped in front of the television. If you give the average Upright five meals a day, with nibbles in between, he'll get fat. That's exactly what can happen to cats. (This doesn't happen to me, of course. My extra weight is largely water. And besides, any excess weight I might carry is down to a slight hormone imbalance for which I cannot possibly be blamed.)

I don't know who first suggested that all cats love milk and should drink it every day – probably some long forgotten advertising Upright working for the Milk Marketing Board. I quite like cows' milk but I know lots of cats who can't stand the stuff. Would you expect a cow to drink cats' milk? Cats don't need milk and it can cause terrible (and sometimes embarrassing) tummy upsets. A lick or two every now and again is fine. But water is much more acceptable, thank you very much.

If I had a mouse for every time I've heard that a cat uses its whiskers to help it balance I would have enough to last me nine lifetimes. We use our whiskers as 'feelers' – to help us gauge whether or not we can get through a narrow gap. But they have nothing to do with our natural balancing skill – that's just down to innate genius.

If I could find the Upright who first claimed that cats always land on their feet and can always survive falls from high places I would throw him out of an aeroplane without a parachute.

We do always try to land feet first and I personally know lots of cats who have managed to survive quite terrifying falls. But (and please remember the 'but' because it's important) cats can be seriously injured – or killed – if they fall. None of us like to admit this but even the most sure-footed cat may get distracted and lose his balance occasionally.

Several otherwise seemingly sane Uprights of my acquaintance seem convinced that putting garlic on a cat's food will get rid of worms. I have no idea where they got this daft idea from.

Personally, I like French cuisine and like many 'chats' from 'La France' I enjoy an occasional sprinkling of garlic on my dinner. But I don't kid myself it's helping to get rid of any worms. I hate to say this (and I'll deny it if you repeat it) but the best way to get rid of worms is to get some medicine from the v-e-t. (Sorry, I have to spell it out. I can't write down the word any more than I can say it out loud.)

Finally, there is a myth that cats who live indoors are immune to disease. This is dangerous rubbish. Uprights can bring germs and bugs into the house on their shoes and clothes. And all sorts of nasties can blow in through the window. Cats who spend all their lives indoors are less likely to get run over. But they're still prone to the same sort of infections that can affect outdoor cats.

About the author
Marmalade is an 8-year-old tortoiseshell who lives in Carmarthenshire, Wales. She is fond of salmon, field mice and custard (though not necessarily together) and has successfully trained a family of five Uprights to pander to her every whim. At the 2001 Catolympics she won a gold medal in the 'Fifty-yard-dash-into-the-house-to-drop-a-mouse-in-the-bedroom-without-being-seen' event.

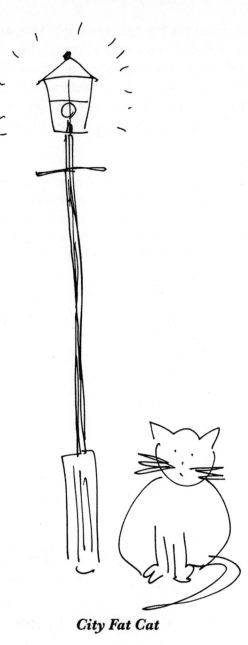

City Fat Cat

The Cat Had Got His Tongue

Cat-kins

4
Catfacts

A collection of curious facts about cats.

☙ Catfact 1

Cats do not have a collarbone. This anatomical peculiarity allows a cat to fit through any opening which is the size of its head.

🐾 Catfact 2
Cats' hearing is much more sensitive than that of humans and dogs. (Cats' hearing stops at 65 khz whereas humans' hearing stops at 20 khz)

🐾 Catfact 3
Give your cat fresh water at least once a day. If your cat refuses your tap water, it may be sensing (with its superior sense of smell) the chlorine or other minerals in your water. Many finicky felines demand bottled water, just like their human counterparts

🐾 Catfact 4
In ancient Egypt the penalty for killing a cat was death.

🐾 Catfact 5
The cat-o'nine-tails was a whip which was used for flogging violent delinquents (in and out of the armed forces) up until 1948 in the UK. The whip consisted of nine thongs of leather which didn't resemble cats' tails very much.

🐾 Catfact 6
Cats purr when they are feeling any intense emotion – whether it is pleasure or pain.

🐾 Catfact 7
Cats have excellent night vision but cannot see in total darkness.

Cat Nap

❀ Catfact 8
Cats may often seem laid-back but they are truly hot-blooded creatures. A cat's normal body temperature is 102 degrees F – several degrees warmer than a human being.

❀ Catfact 9
When running flat out a domestic cat can reach 31 miles per hour.

❀ Catfact 10
Cats can be identified by their nose pads. Every cat's nose pad is unique. No two nose prints are the same.

❀ Catfact 11
The collective noun for a brood or litter of kittens is a 'kindle'.

❀ Catfact 12
If you are stressed you may be able to lower your blood pressure a little by stroking a cat.

❧ Catfact 13
A cat can jump 5 times as high as its height. So, a cat that is one foot tall can jump five feet up into the air.

❧ Catfact 14
Cats have eighteen toes – five toes on each front paw, but only four toes on each back paw.

❧ Catfact 15
Cats are great contortionists. Their forelegs can turn in almost any direction and the two halves of their bodies can move in opposite directions.

❧ Catfact 16
Cats have two coats of fur – an undercoat and an outer coat.

❧ Catfact 17
A female cat can have between three and seven kittens at four monthly intervals.

❧ Catfact 18
The phrase 'to be made a cat's paw of' (which means to serve as a tool for someone else) comes from Aesop's fable of a monkey who used the paw of his friend, the cat, to pull hot chestnuts out of a fire.

❧ Catfact 19
Cats are social animals. They really do respond and answer to speech, and enjoy human companionship. The more cats are spoken to, the more they will speak to you.

❧ Catfact 20
Cats usually prefer their food to be served at room temperature. They will often refuse to eat food that is too cold or too hot.

❧ Catfact 21
A cat cannot see directly down. (This is why cats can't see pieces of food which are lying on the floor right under their noses.)

❧ Catfact 22
Cats get a sense of security from hearing the voice of someone they know. So talking to your cat isn't daft. The tone of voice is important. A cat will know if you're yelling at him or her.

❧ Catfact 23
Ten Cat Loving Artists and Composers

1. Borodin
2. Chopin
3. Debussy

4. Manet
5. Matisse
6. Picasso
7. Ravel
8. Stravinsky
9. Tchaikovsky
10. Warhol

😺 Catfact 24

The catflap was invented by cat-lover Sir Isaac Newton (famous for the apple and the laws of gravity) who was worried about the fact that his pet cats couldn't get in and out of his house whenever they wanted to. It was Sir Isaac who first thought of putting a small cat door within the larger, human door. Sir Isaac also invented the kitten-flap. When his cat had kittens who weren't strong enough to push open the flap Sir Isaac had a smaller hole (with a smaller flap) specially made for them.

😺 Catfact 25

People who are allergic to cats are some-times more allergic to male cats than female cats – and least likely to be al-lergic to spayed female cats.

😺 Catfact 26

Texas tabby cat named Dusty had 420 kittens. She had her last litter at the age of 18.

Aristocat

🐾 Catfact 27

Cats regard Uprights as huge, overgrown cats. This explains much of their behaviour.

Rat-a-cat-rat

Catfact 28
Cats are subject to gum disease and to dental caries. They should have their teeth professionally cleaned by a vet once a year.

Catfact 29
Cats with white fur and skin on their ears are prone to sunburn – which can lead to skin cancer. White cats may need surgery to remove all or part of a cancerous ear. Preventive measures include sunscreen, or better still, keeping the cat indoors in sunny weather.

Catfact 30
A cat is pregnant for roughly two months.

Catfact 31
There are more than 500 million domestic cats in the world – divided amongst 33 different breeds.

Catfact 32
The largest cat breed is the Ragdoll. Fully grown males weigh twelve to twenty pounds and fully grown females weigh ten to fifteen pounds.

Catfact 33
Most cats have no eyelashes.

Catfact 34
Many cats cannot properly digest cows' milk with the result that milk and milk products may give them diarrhoea.

Catfact 35
Bluebell, a Persian cat living in South Africa, gave birth to 14 kittens in one litter – all of whom survived.

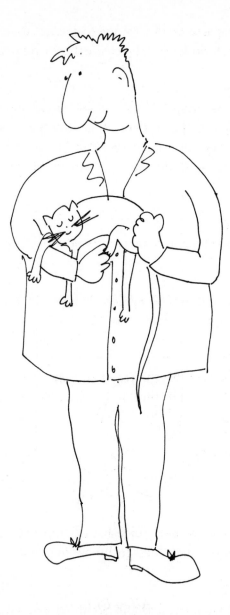

Alley Cat

Having a bad day

Cat-a-tonic (1)

😺 Catfact 36
An English cat called Puss died in 1939 just one day after her 36th birthday.

😺 Catfact 37
American tough guy author Ernest Hemingway shared his life with 30 cats, including F. Puss; Thruster; Dillinger; Furhouse; Willy; Fats; Crazy Christian; Friendless Brother and Ecstasy.

😺 Catfact 38
Cats are attracted by movement when they are hunting. But finding out which prey is food, and which is just a ball of paper on a piece of string, is learned behaviour.

Cat Heaven

☙ Catfact 39
In the early 1960s a pair of cats inherited over £200,000. The richest single cat is a white alley cat who inherited £180,000.

☙ Catfact 40
The smallest cat breed is the Singapura. Adult males usually weigh about six pounds while adult females weigh about four pounds.

☙ Catfact 41
Twenty-Five Famous Authors Who Loved Cats:

1. Honore de Balzac
2. Emily Brontë
3. Lord Byron
4. Raymond Chandler
5. Jean Cocteau
6. Colette
7. Charles Dickens
8. Alexander Dumas
9. Anatole France
10. Thomas Hardy
11. Ernest Hemingway
12. Victor Hugo
13. Aldous Huxley
14. Henry James
15. Jerome K.Jerome
16. Samuel Johnson
17. Rudyard Kipling
18. Guy de Maupassant
19. Dorothy L Sayers
20. Sir Walter Scott
21. William Makepeace Thackeray

22. Mark Twain
23. Horace Walpole
24. H.G. Wells
25. Emile Zola

☻ Catfact 42
Cats can make 100 different vocal sounds. (Dogs
can manage only ten.)

☻ Catfact 43
Tinker Toy, a male Himalayan-Persian, weighed
one pound eight ounces when fully grown. He was seven and a
quarter inches long and two and three quarter inches tall!

☻ Catfact 44
If a cat sleeps with all four paws tucked underneath him or her
it means that cold weather is coming (possibly).

☻ Catfact 45
Wild cats and big cats hold their tails horizontally, or between
their legs, when they are walking. The domestic cat is the only
species of cat which is able to hold its tail vertically while walking.

☻ Catfact 46
A cat cannot move its jaw sideways.

☻ Catfact 47
Cats have a third eyelid which is rarely visible.

☻ Catfact 48
Most tortoiseshell cats are female. The only exceptions are
occasional, sterile males.

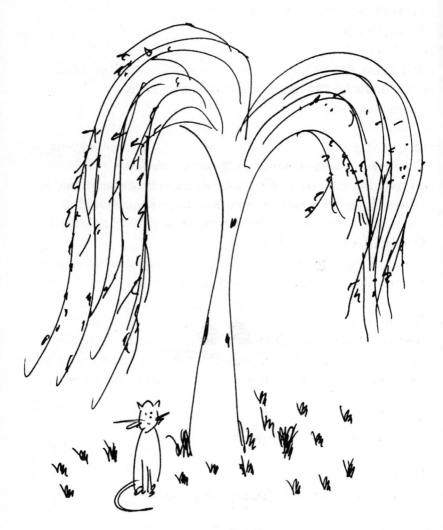

Pussy Willow

☙ Catfact 49
In 1950 a four-month-old kitten followed a group of Alpine climbers to the top of the Matterhorn.

☙ Catfact 50
A cat has 32 muscles in each ear – that's an impressive 64 ear muscles for a fully equipped and operational moggie.

☙ Catfact 51
Florence Nightingale, the 'Lady of the Lamp', and the founder of modern nursing, owned 60 cats during her lifetime. All her cats were large Persians. Florence, who refused to travel anywhere without her current favourites, named her cats after the famous men of her day. So, for example, she had three cats called Disraeli, Gladstone and Bismarck.

Cool Cat

😺 Catfact 52

Cats, camels and giraffes may not seem to have much in common but they all walk by moving their front and back right legs together (and then moving the legs on the left side together too).

😺 Catfact 53

The cat is the only domestic animal which doesn't get a mention in the Bible.

😺 Catfact 54

In relation to body size cats have the largest eyes of any mammal.

Copy Cats

❧ Catfact 55

There is a myth that the first cat appeared when Noah, afraid that the rats might eat all the food on the ark, prayed to God for help. God responded by making the lion sneeze. When the lion sneezed he produced a small cat.

❧ Catfact 56

Mark Twain's cats were called: Sour Mash; Apollinaris; Zoroaster and Blatherskite.

❧ Catfact 57

The first cats appeared 40,000,000 years ago. This makes cats one of the oldest mammalian families.

❧ Catfact 58

Ailurophilia means the love of cats. Many famous people, especially authors, can be described as ailurophiles.

❧ Catfact 59

Frederic Chopin's *Cat Waltz* (opus 34. no.3) was partially inspired by his pet cat, which bravely jumped onto his keyboard while he was composing.

❧ Catfact 60

The average cat has 130,000 hairs per square inch. This explains why your cat can leave cat hairs everywhere without going bald.

☙ Catfact 61

Ailurophobia means the fear of cats. Some ailurophobes cannot bear to be touched by cats, others can't bear to be in the same room. Many are frightened that a cat will jump up on them unexpectedly.

☙ Catfact 62

Cats are perfect hunting animals. They have powerful jaws, long, sharp teeth, and retractible claws. They have excellent hearing and eyesight which is particularly good in the dim light just before dawn and just after dusk, the best periods for hunting.

☙ Catfact 63
Cat Loving Stars

1. Fred Astaire
2. Tallulah Bankhead
3. Brigitte Bardot
4. Warren Beatty
5. Doris Day
6. Charles Laughton
7. Robert De Niro
8. Edward G. Robinson
9. Elizabeth Taylor
10. Franco Zeffirelli

☙ Catfact 64

The popular belief that a cat has nine lives first became widespread in 1546.

Reigning Cats and Dogs

Cat-a-pillar

Cataholic

😺 Catfact 65

A female cat called Mincho, who lived in Argentina, went up a tree and stayed there for six years. While living up the tree she managed to have three litters of kittens.

😺 Catfact 66
Other words for 'cat'

1. French   *chat (m)/chatte (f)*
2. German   *katze/katti/ket*
3. Irish   *cat/cait*
4. Italian   *gatto (m)/gatta (f)*
5. Japanese   *neko*
6. Norwegian   *katt (m)/katta (f)*
7. Russian   *kot (m)/kotchka/koshka (f)*
8. Scottish   *catti*
9. Spanish   *gato (m)/gata (f)*
10. Welsh   *cath/kath/cetti*

😺 Catfact 67

Lord Byron had five cats which travelled with him around Europe.

😺 Catfact 68

Egyptians used to shave their eyebrows, as a sign of mourning, when a favourite cat died.

😺 Catfact 69

In Wellington, New Zealand, a tom cat called Maurice is reported to have a penchant for – and an impressive collection

of – ladies' underwear. Maurice has so far acquired 60 items of underwear, including a particularly impressive collection of bras.

☙ Catfact 70
After the former leader, Screaming Lord Sutch, died, a four-year-old ginger tom cat called Mandu was elected joint leader of the Monster Raving Loony Party – a political party in the UK. Mandu received as many votes as the leading Upright candidate for the leadership of the party.

☙ Catfact 71
Sir Winston Churchill, Britain's Prime Minister during the Second World War, adored cats. Both in the Cabinet Room and at the dining table, the chair next to him was reserved for his favourite cat. The main occupant of these chairs was a black cat from Admiralty House named Nelson who also shared Churchill's bed. Churchill insisted that by acting as a hot water bottle, and therefore saving fuel, Nelson was helping the war effort.

Playing cat and mouse

🐾 Catfact 72

Alexander the Great, Julius Caesar and Napoleon Bonaparte were all terrified of cats.

🐾 Catfact 73

Cats tend to have shorter lives than people – and to age more rapidly. The following table shows (roughly) how old a cat is in human terms.

- The cat who is 1 year old is 15 years old in human years.
- The cat who is 2 years old is 25 years old in human years.
- The cat who is 4 years old is 40 years old in human years.
- The cat who is 7 years old is 50 years old in human years.
- The cat who is 10 years old is 60 years old in human years.

Cat Fish

- The cat who is 15 years old is 75 years old in human years.
- The cat who is 20 years old is 105 years old in human years.
- The cat who is 30 years old is 120 years old in human years.

😺 Catfact 74
The phrase 'to grin like a Cheshire cat' means to grin from ear to ear and comes from Lewis Carroll's book *Alice in Wonderland*. No one seems to know where Lewis Carroll got the idea from – and he's not telling.

😺 Catfact 75
More than nine out of ten cat owners admit that they talk to their cats.

😺 Catfact 76
The Most Popular Names For Cats

1. Sooty
2. Ginger
3. Blackie
4. Smokey
5. Tom
6. Tigger
7. Fluffy
8. Tiger
9. Timmy
10. Marmalade

😺 Catfact 77
The Ten Most Popular Sayings Involving Cats
(The date in brackets refers to the estimated origin of the saying.)

1. When the cat's away the mice will play. (1470)
2. A cat may look at a king. (1546)

3. Be careful not to let the cat out of the bag. (1760)
4. That's put the cat among the pigeons. (1706)
5. Watch which way the cat jumps. (1825)
6. An old cat laps as much milk as a young one. (1605)
7. A baited cat may grow as fierce as a lion. (1620)
8. The cat would eat fish but would not wet her feet. (1225)
9. As the cat plays with the mouse. (1340)
10. A cat in gloves catches no mice. (1573)

😺 Catfact 78
French writer Colette had cats called: Petiteu; Kiki-la-Doucette; Saha; Mini-mini; Kapok; Kro; Muscat; La Touteu; Franchette; Zwerg; Pinichette; Ba-tou; Minionne; Toune; La Chatte; One and only and finally, and appropriately, La Chatte Dernière.

Cat-a-logs

Fat Cat (1)

Scaredy Cat

"I see it's just raining cats today"

Puss in Boot

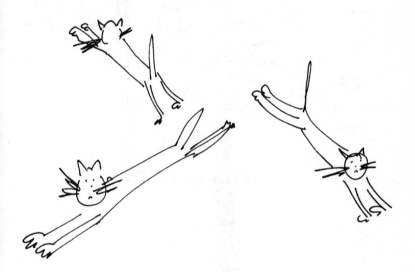

S – cat – tter

Cat-amaran

Cat-isfaction

Cat Nip

5
Cat Tales
A collection of limericks and poems about cats.

Cat Tale 1

A pretty young pussy called Kate
Chased rabbits all day until late
    She caught quite a few
    And ate one or two
But never put on any weight.

Cat Tale 2

A jolly young kitten called Thom
Went out for a walk with her Mom
She ran up a tree
While chasing a bee
And was saved in the end by Anon.

Cat Tale 3

I love my little kitten
She's cute and small and white
She loves to lie upon my bed
And stay there all the night

When sunshine lights the room
And a new day has begun
I'm reminded very soon
That she's the chosen one

Her tiny little paws
So small and cute and neat
Are the unrelenting cause
Of my stumbling to my feet.

Cat Tale 4

A black and white kitten called Spot
Caused trouble, all day, quite a lot.
He fell down the stairs,
Scratched all the chairs,
And loved the attention he got.

Cat Tale 5

Two pretty young tabbies called Tiddles
Liked fish but only the middles
They claimed they were poor
When eaten quite raw
So they baked them at home on their griddles.

Cat Tale 6

A playful young kitten called Tate
Stayed out of the house very late

He played in the dark
In a nearby park
And his Uprights had a long wait.

Cat Tale 7

A grizzled old Tom cat called Len
Went out every night after ten
He played with the boys
And made lots of noise
And did it again and again.

Cat Tale 8

A long-haired Persian called Kate
Ate everything put on her plate
She loved herrings and salmon and a good thick fish stew
And milk and custard and lots of cheese too
She nibbled and licked and swallowed and chewed
And her habits when eating were often quite rude
Sometimes folk pointed and remarked on her weight
But she simply replied it was all down to fate.

Cat Tale 9

A four-week-old kitten called Trouble
Was found in a field of stubble
The Upright who found her then found another
A sweet little kitten, clearly her brother
And then there were two and the trouble was double.

Cat Tale 10

A jolly old woman from Crete
Had a pretty young pussy called Pete
They had a house by the sea
Ate fresh salmon with tea
And occasionally had cream as a treat.

"How did that get there?"

Russian Cats

Cat Tale 11

A sleepy old pussy called Garth
Spent all day stretched out by the hearth
He twitched as he slept and chased lots of rabbits
and because he was old he had some strange habits
But everyone smiled as he
stayed by the fire
And they threw on more
logs to make the flames
higher
'Look how relaxed dear old
Garth is,' they'd say
'Nothing whatever will
disturb him today.'

Cat Tale 12

A handsome old tom cat called Tim
Was not fat but was also not thin
He lived by the sea and ate lots of fish
Which he often declared was his favourite dish
His fur was jet black and he always looked well
If you asked him just why, he would happily tell:
'It's simple, you see, I don't mind the smell,
I eat lots of fish. That's why I look well.'

Cat Tale 13

A happy young cat known as Kitty
Was really exceptionally pretty.
She caught lots of mice
(Which she thought were quite nice)
In the house where she lived in the city.

Cat Tale 14

A rumbustious wee kitten from Wales
Was purchased quite cheap in the sales
The couple who bought him
Had been out a courtin'
And were fond of small creatures with tails.

Cat Tale 15

A pretty young cat from Kent
Lived in a very large tent
It was cosy inside
A nice place to hide
And a very affordable rent.

Cat Tale 16

There was a young wild cat from Leicester
Who lived with a tabby called Hector
They stayed out late at nights
And got into fights
With a Tom cat who came down from Chester.

Cat Tale 17

A saucy young kitten
called Dot
Was proud of the whiskers
she'd got.
They were long and quite fine
And looked most divine.
So she loved them a hell of a lot.

Cat Tale 18

A tough ginger tom called Curry
When tickled ran off in a hurry.
'I know it seems odd for a puss,
But I really don't like too much fuss.'
He told a reporter called Murray.

Stunt Cat

"You'd think they'd never seen two cats on bicycles before."

A cat may look at a king

No room to swing a cat

Cat's cradle

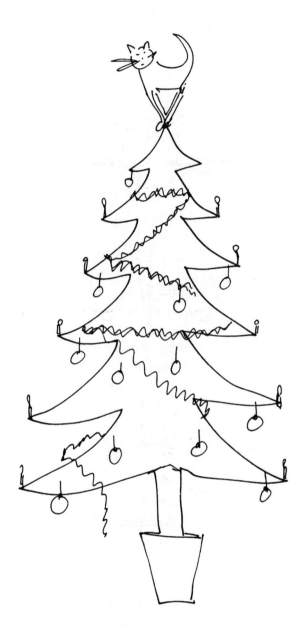

Cat Suit

Fat Cat (2)

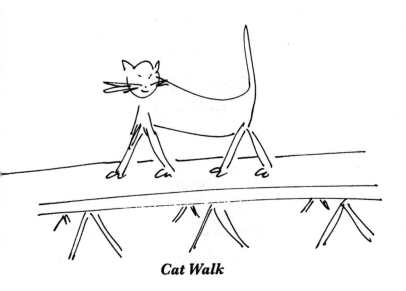

Cat Walk

The Cat's Pyjamas

Cat's Eye

6
Favourite hiding places

Cats love to hide. I invited two cats to contribute lists of their favourite hiding places.

Muffy's Ten Favourite Hiding Places

1. In the airing cupboard.
2. In the bed.
3. In the laundry basket.
4. Behind the sofa.
5. In the washing machine (until anxious Uprights started making sure that the door was always kept closed).
6. Underneath the bed.
7. At the back of the wardrobe.
8. On top of the wardrobe.
9. In the bath (when empty!).
10. On a pile of overalls and gardening clothes in the garage.

Muffy is a 6-year-old orange tabby.

Sniffy's Ten Favourite Hiding Places

1. In the airing cupboard.
2. In the laundry basket (only when full of clean laundry).
3. On top of old sacks, in the potting shed.
4. On top of the bookcase.
5. In the cellar.
6. In the lawnmower grass box.
7. Anywhere in the attic.
8. In the broom cupboard.
9. On top of the wardrobe.
10. Underneath the spare bed.

Sniffy is a 4-year-old mackerel tabby.

7
Quotes About Cats

'A man waits on a cat hand and foot for weeks, humouring its lightest whim, and it goes and leaves him flat because it has found a place down the road where fish is more frequent.'
P.G. Wodehouse

'She sits composedly sentinel, with paws tucked under her a good part of her days at present, by some ridiculous little hole, the possible entry of a mouse.'
Henry David Thoreau

'There are no ordinary cats.'
Colette

Something the cat brought in

'I am enough of a cat lover to be suspicious of a household that doesn't have a cat...'
Kingsley Amis

'I love cats because I love my home, and after a while they become its visible soul.'
Jean Cocteau

'He will kill mice and he will be kind to babies...but when the moon gets up and the night comes, he is the Cat who Walks by Himself.'
Rudyard Kipling

'Even the smallest feline is a work of art.'
Leonardo Da Vinci

'No matter how much cats fight, there always seem to be plenty of kittens.'
Abraham Lincoln

Cat-a-tonic (2)

Cat-astrophe

'You haven't lived until you have lived with a cat.'
Doris Day

'The cat has complete emotional honesty – an attribute not often found in humans.'
Ernest Hemingway

'I learned a vital lesson of life from a little kitten of mine. When approached aggressively by my biggest cat the kitten stood her ground. When the old enemy came near enough she kissed his nose and made peace. That is the lesson of life; to kiss one's enemy's nose, always standing one's ground.'
Florence Nightingale

'There is no doubt that it is very flattering when a cat jumps on to your lap.'
Kingsley Amis

Cat Among the Pigeons

'If a man could be crossed with a cat, it would improve man but it would deteriorate the cat.'
Mark Twain

'A kitten is so flexible that she is almost double; the hind parts are equivalent to another kitten with which the forepart plays. She does not discover that her tail belongs to her until you tread on it.'
Henry David Thoreau

'If you want to write, keep cats.'
Aldous Huxley

We know you will have enjoyed *We Love Cats*. And now we'd like to introduce you to Alice, a mixed tabby cat who is the author of two international best-selling books. Her first book, *Alice's Diary*, takes us through one eventful year in her all too short life. Alice was much loved by all those who knew her and who were lucky enough to share her life. She was a companion who gave nothing but love and joy to those around her and she is missed every day. Thankfully, she can live on in her books which have so far entertained many thousands of readers around the world. Here are a few pages for you to enjoy.

January 1st

Thomasina and I got into terrible trouble last night. We wandered into the kitchen early in the evening and found a huge plateful of delicious sandwiches on the table. We ate the middles out of half a dozen and then the Upright in Trousers came into the room. He shouted and threw a towel at us.

To avoid further trouble Thomasina and I left and went outside.

From underneath the lilac tree we then watched an apparently endless stream of visitors arrive. They were all elegantly dressed, they parked their cars all over the lawn and they carried gifts with them. Our Uprights were clearly having a party of some kind.

Thomasina suggested that in order to make our peace with the Upright in Trousers we should take in a small gift of our own. So I caught a plump and rather succulent looking fieldmouse and Thomasina picked up a bedraggled looking vole with a limp.

I don't think one should ever expect too much enthusiasm when arriving with a gift but I have to admit that we were both rather startled by the reception we got. The Upright who wears a Skirt started to scream and jumped up onto a chair. Someone else knocked over a tray full of glasses and a strange Upright whom I'd never seen before fainted. The Upright in Trousers then completely spoiled the mood of what promised to be a spectacular party by chasing the pair of us round the living room and threatening Thomasina with a large ladle.

In the end Thomasina and I decided that it was all far too exciting for us. We left our presents and went outside to spend the rest of the night in the garage.

When we woke up this morning all the cars had gone

and it was raining. I hate rain. Rain means mud.

I hate mess too and the inside of the house was in a terrible state. There were at least a dozen empty bottles lying on the floor in the living room and piles of dirty cups, plates and glasses in the kitchen. The sink was absolutely overflowing with them. Worst of all our food dish was quite empty.

Showing a remarkable level of patience both Thomasina and I sat and waited.

After two hours of hunger we crept upstairs to where the Uprights sleep. Normally I can wake them easily. A purr in the ear will usually do the trick. But they were both sleeping far too soundly to be woken so easily.

Full of despair, but absolutely empty of food, Thomasina and I went back downstairs again and made our way through into the kitchen. The plate of sandwiches that we'd started the night before was still sitting on the kitchen table. The pile was by no means as high as it had been the previous evening but there were still a dozen or so sandwiches waiting to be eaten. Desperate with hunger we jumped up onto the table and started to help ourselves.

Unfortunately, the plate was rather close to the edge and in our haste and excitement we knocked it off onto the floor. The crash was terrifyingly loud. Thomasina and I froze. At first I thought we might have got away with it but after a couple of minutes the Upright in Trousers came staggering downstairs in his pyjamas. I expected him to be furious but he looked at the plateful of scattered sandwiches and the broken plate, bent down and rubbed the side of my neck, murmured something affectionate and then went back upstairs again leaving us to help ourselves to the sandwiches!

Thomasina and I looked at one another and shrugged. I've never understood Uprights and I don't think I ever will.

January 2nd

The Uprights who live next door have acquired a dog.
For the first few days the creature paid us remarkably
little attention but slowly he has become bolder. Yester-
day he barked persistently every time we went out into
the garden. He terrified my half sister Thomasina who
has always been rather frightened by dogs.

Today I decided that the dog must be taught a lesson.
So while Thomasina stayed indoors well out of the way
I went down to the bottom of the garden and sat on a
fence post where it could see me.

Inevitably the dog's response was to try and jump up
and catch me. But since the fence post was five feet up
in the air I was perfectly safe.

I stayed up there for twenty minutes or so to get the
dog in quite a rage and then I jumped down onto the
flower border on our side of the fence. Just at this point
there is a small hole in the fence, nowhere near large
enough for a dog to get through but plenty large enough
for him to use as a peep hole.

Naturally the dog got even more excited when he saw
that I was down at ground level. He barked, scratched
and whined and did a considerable amount of damage
to the flower border on his side of the fence.

Eventually one of the neighbouring Uprights came
down the garden path to see what was the matter. When
he saw the mess that the dog had made he was absolutely
furious. Through the fence I heard the dog whimpering
pitifully.

Thomasina has been well avenged.

January 3rd

The dog next door has now been tethered to a large stake
in the centre of the lawn. I spent a pleasant half an hour
running up and down the top of the fence between our

gardens. The stupid animal tried to follow me but ended up winding his lead round and round the stake. After thirty minutes the dog's lead was no more than a yard long and the wretched animal had become a prisoner of his own stupidity. Eventually I just sat while he barked and whimpered.

"I sat while the dog barked and whimpered."

I am glad that I am not a dog. They are such unintelligent animals.

January 4th

A good day today. I caught two mice, a shrew and a vole with a squint.

Price £9.95 (hardback) • Published by Chilton Designs
Order from: Publishing House • Trinity Place • Barnstaple •
Devon EX32 9HJ • England • Tel 01271 328892 • Fax 01271 328768

Alice and Other Friends

When Alice had to leave us (a victim of oral cancer), Vernon wrote this book in her memory. Here are a couple of sample pages.

Thomasina writes

Thomasina walked across my computer keyboard one morning. In order to print something which appears on the screen it is necessary to press two keys simultaneously. The keys are about 20 cm apart on the keyboard. Somehow Thomasina succeeded in pressing them both and her work was duly printed.

Here is what she wrote.

999999999999999990000000000000877777yhojsadgtAxcv rmuhbtttttttttttttttttttttttttttttttttttttttttttttttttttttttttg vrdeeeeeeeeeeeeeeeeeeeeeeeeeeeeeeeeeee3222222222222222qa2AAAAAAAA A A A A A A A A A A A A 2 2 2 2 2 2 2 2 2 2 2 2 2 2 2 IUUUUUUUUUUUUUUUUUUU.

Maybe Thomasina should apply for a government grant to continue her work. But there again she is probably too intelligent to receive a government grant.

Not fair!

Alice had a bad foot one day. The vet told us that we had to keep her in. She was very unhappy about staying in. She kept looking at me as if to say: 'It's not fair. I've got a bad foot AND I'm being kept in.'

"Alice kept looking at me as if to say 'Its not fair! I've got a bad foot AND I'm being kept in!' "

Alice on my knees

I wrote the two 'Alice' books with Alice sitting on my knees. She enjoyed being with me as I wrote or typed. I always felt that Alice really did 'write' the books and I always thought of them as her books. She even sat on my lap when I did some of the illustrations. I had to throw away many attempts because she had nudged me while I was drawing.

"I 'wrote' the two 'Alice' books with the author sitting on my knees."

Price £12.95 (hardback) • Published by Chilton Designs
Order from: Publishing House • Trinity Place • Barnstaple •
Devon EX32 9HJ • England • Tel 01271 328892 • Fax 01271 328768

Also by Vernon Coleman

Alice's Adventures

After the publication of her first book Alice was inundated with fan mail and requests urging her to put pen to paper once more. The result is this, her second volume of memoirs.

In her second book she records yet more adventures and mishaps with many a tear being shed during this eventful year.

Full of the illustrations and humour so much-loved by readers of her first book.

"I didn't think Alice could surpass her first book – but she has. I really loved Alice's Adventures. The saddest moment came when I finished it. When will the next volume be ready?"
(Mrs K., Somerset)

"We have had cats for over 30 years and Alice describes incidents which are so real that we nearly died laughing at them."
(Mrs O., Leeds)

"Alice's Adventures is the loveliest book I have ever read. It captures everything brilliantly. Thinking back over the book I can't help smiling. I have never enjoyed a book as much."
(Mrs H., Edinburgh)

Price £9.95 (hardback)

Published by Chilton Designs
Order from Publishing House • Trinity Place • Barnstaple • Devon EX32 9HJ • England
Telephone 01271 328892 • Fax 01271 328768

Also by Vernon Coleman

The Bilbury Chronicles

A young doctor arrives to begin work in the small village of Bilbury. This picturesque hamlet is home to some memorable characters who have many a tale to tell, and Vernon Coleman weaves together a superb story full of humour and anecdotes. The Bilbury books will transport you back to the days of old-fashioned, traditional village life where you never needed to lock your door, and when a helping hand was only ever a moment away. The first novel in the series.

"I am just putting pen to paper to say how very much I enjoyed The Bilbury Chronicles. I just can't wait to read the others."
(Mrs K., Cambs)

"...a real delight from cover to cover. As the first in a series it holds out the promise of entertaining things to come."
(Daily Examiner)

"The Bilbury novels are just what I've been looking for. They are a pleasure to read over and over again."
(Mrs C., Lancs)

Price £12.95 (hardback)

Published by Chilton Designs
Order from Publishing House • Trinity Place • Barnstaple •
Devon EX32 9HJ • England
Telephone 01271 328892 • Fax 01271 328768

Also by Vernon Coleman

Second Innings

The characters leap from the page as they draw you in to this tale of a young man (Biffo Brimstone) who overcomes the adversity of modern day living by, quite simply, running away! He leaves an unrewarding job, a shrewish and demanding wife and a couple of surly children and takes the next train out of the miserable suburban estate which has been his home for the past few years of his mundane life.

The train takes him to a part of the country he has never before visited, and the subsequent bus journey deposits him in the village of Fondling-under-Water. It is there that his new life begins.

"A piece of good old-fashioned escapism, an easy-to-follow plot; just right to relax with after a busy day ... you would be happy to lend it to your granny or anyone else's granny come to that. This author has the ability to create a distinctive 'mind's eye' picture of every character. The story would 'translate' into an excellent radio play."
(The Journal of the Cricket Society)

"Settling down with Vernon Coleman's latest novel is one of the best restorative treatments I know for relieving the stresses and strains of modern living. Right from page one you can feel yourself unwind as you enjoy the antics of the wonderful array of characters and their exploits. Terrific reading for anyone." *(Lincolnshire Echo)*

Price £14.95 (hardback)

Published by Chilton Designs
Order from Publishing House • Trinity Place • Barnstaple •
Devon EX32 9HJ • England
Telephone 01271 328892 • Fax 01271 328768

Also by Vernon Coleman

It's Never Too Late

Tony Davison is bored, tired and fed up with life. He has lost his job and his wife, and doesn't have much of a future. In despair, he sells his house and most of his belongings and sets off to Paris for a weekend holiday. But what started off as a quick holiday break soon turns into a once-in-a-lifetime experience.

It's Never Too Late tells the uplifting story of Tony's search for a new life and happiness in a new country. Full of the gentle humour and anecdotes which are so much the hallmark of Vernon Coleman's novels.

"Imagine that you feel like settling down in a comfortable armchair with an entertaining book – one that will keep your attention and combat the desire to nod off ... If this description fits you then you could do much worse than spoil yourself with this book. The author's style is both easy to read and makes you want to keep turning the pages – in fact I had to force myself to stop reading and put the book down. I am sure you will enjoy the book, which apart from anything else brings to life the atmosphere of Paris – so why not give it to a loved one or friend ... and promptly borrow it to read yourself!? Whatever you may decide, we have chosen this as our Book of the Month." *(Living France)*

"It's Never Too Late is a light-hearted reversal of the ageing process." *(France Magazine)*

Price £14.95 (hardback)

Published by Chilton Designs
Order from Publishing House • Trinity Place • Barnstaple •
Devon EX32 9HJ • England
Telephone 01271 328892 • Fax 01271 328768

For a catalogue of Vernon Coleman's books
please write to:

Publishing House
Trinity Place
Barnstaple
Devon EX32 9HJ
England

Telephone   01271 328892
Fax   01271 328768

Outside the UK:
Telephone   +44 1271 328892
Fax   +44 1271 328768

Or visit our website:

www.vernoncoleman.com